BEIRUT AGAIN

BEIRUT AGAIN

poems by Allen C. West

Allen C. West

Phil, I hope you enjoy these poems. with best wishes, Al

11/7/14
Lexington, MA

Off the Grid Press
Somerville, Massachusetts

Published by:

Off the Grid Press
24 Quincy Street
Somerville, MA 02143
www.offthegridpress.net

ACKNOWLEDGMENTS

These poems have appeared, or will appear, some under different titles, some in different forms, in the following publications:

The Antigonish Review: "Poem for My Birthday"
The Aurorean: "The Ridge of Shouf," "Making a Map"
Brooklyn Review: "Touch"
The Comstock Review: "Ghost," "Being Five," "Terse Biography of My Father"
Concrete Wolf: "Poem for My Birthday"
English Journal: "Black Bag," "Solitaire"
Fox Cry Review: "The River's Edge"
Hawaii Pacific Review: "Leaving Beirut"
The Larcom Review: "False Dawn"
The Mid-America Poetry Review: "Making Jelly Alone," "Pilgrim," "Aubade," "The Rope"
on line, *The Noble Beast:* "When I get home I"
Passager: "Everything Is Happening Again," "Dancing While Sweeping"
Pudding: "Leaving Beirut"
RHINO: "The Wild Iris"
Rockhurst Review: "Paradox"
Salamander: "Periscope"
Sanctuary: "Spring with Two Crows"
The Senior Times: "beloved," "Amber"

"The Time of Ripe Figs" won the chapbook competition of the *White Eagle Coffee Store Press* in 2001 and was published in 2002. The following poems, some under different titles, some in different forms, appeared in it: "Everything Is Happening Again," "Even if It Might," "I Comforted Her with Apples," "Solitaire," "Pas de Deux," "After Breakfast," "The Tumbler," "False Dawn," "Amber," "beloved," "When I get home I," "I Find Her," "Black Bag," "The River's Edge," "At the Fountain," "Ghost," "Lost," "Down the Street of Sleep," "Making Jelly Alone," "About the Changes and So Much More Unchanged," "Poem for My Birthday."

I am grateful to my editors Tam Neville and Bert Stern at *Off the Grid Press* for their comments, a fresh point of view, and many suggestions that improved the manuscript; to friends who have shared my poetry and helped make it better, especially all those in The Workshop for Publishing Poets; and, particularly, to Barbara Helfgott Hyett, its director, who deserves my special thanks. Without her unsparing criticism and continuous support *Beirut Again* would never have come this far.

Cover photograph, "Cedar Tree, Lebanon," © Ddkg/Dreamstime.com.
Book design by Michael Alpert.

ISBN: 978-0-9778429-4-0

In memory of William A. West, my father
born in Beirut, Lebanon, 1894
died in Kensington, Maryland, 1980

CONTENTS

III.   IN A TIME OF RIPE FIGS

BEIRUT AGAIN

I. THE WHETSTONE

Periscope

We tack on the systoles
of the sea   Beirut becoming
nothing but horizon   our only god
What is slicing the glitter   my father
at the tiller   pointing the way
he does at sudden orchids in a field
Who is watching   Who is trying to
read me like some Rosetta Stone
the war in Spain too far

The black *Jeanne d'Arc*
steams past   all three decks
friezed with faces   Do they see
my mirror bounce the heavy sunlight
a million parsecs pressing on funnels
On the sea floor sea stars make
their own dark heaven   Who
signals back   *Here we are*
We are here

Being Five

I used to sneak out
between the window bars,
out to run among the thyme
and silent pines, the bees there,
and doves in their antiphonal
devotions, the muezzin's
la ilaha illa.

That was the year
I learned to spell my name,
not in cursive's shrunken river,
but my own A alive, my own
2 Ls, the long way to E,
my earthen N,

my pen
the only thing I wanted
after naptime, my name stiff
and spiky, every line straight,
every letter a block, black,
Platonic, by itself.

Trying to Sleep

Dark curdles the oaks
and the stones I dare

to know on the black
wall of the lane.

In bed under netting
my fingers mash

trapped mosquitoes
into bloodied mesh.

Jackals in the valley
wail. Nothing scares me

except shadows
and the murderer waiting

out there. He's come alive
from the detective story.

His whistle will call
back the speckled band.

The Last Syrian Bear

Behind bars, he's a rug,
dirt-brown as mountain
dust, until he lumbers
to his feet full-formed,

a looming bulk, shoulders
humped, and the eyes,
ochre, leveled on mine.
He doesn't show his teeth,

just stands there naked,
not attending to his bowl
of bones. With me alone
he prowls back and forth.

If I stop, he stops. If
I walk, he walks. His snout
sniffs the air, spurning
the smell of his cage,

the clutch of his cage,
and I am the boy
who lives in his mountains,
come down to console him.

The Ridge of Shouf

Morning beats its chest,
Look! Look! Look!
summer's never-failing glare.

Climb Big Rock.
Be King of the Valley.
Wild pine cones spill

across the wooded hillside.
Chinese Checkers, double
solitaire, a train of pencils

derailing on the stones.
Cicadas grind the noon away.
From the olive tree spiders

swing by their knees,
and sulfur yellows, rare
as gold, flutter from my net.

Peer from hiding. Listen!
Shouts of searchers
beseige my thicket.

The Summit

We ate everything
my father carried: four
Zebdani apples, sandwiches
of jam, a chocolate bar,

drank water from the World
War I canteen. Pointing
far to the far blue skim,
It's the sea, he said.

I didn't know. Among
the rocks he found a geode,
took from his pack
his pick-hammer,

cracked open that globe
to show me the crystal
cavern snug-coiled there.
He told me of primes,

1 to 97, divisible only
by themselves or one,
but his mouth was tense
and 97 too far.

After Supper

I swing a bamboo pole
at flitting bats, hit one

like a softball I can't see.
Thunk! I run home

in the dark, throwing rocks
at cats, and climb out

my window, claw the grit,
stand on the roof,

the kite I made under
my arm. I toss it the way

men toss pigeons into wind
that snatches, flings,

the string unwinding
from its sphere, my kite

dancing the Pole Star.
I'm here!

Miss Kitchin

Her chairs wear lace doilies white as the collar
on her black dress. From the bowl on the table

I take a chocolate kiss and slowly flay its foil
skin, smooth it whole into a silver mirror

against a flowered plate with my thumbnail.
Miss Kitchin pours tea. I count the blue lines

that vein her hand. My shirt is too tight, my shirt
is too stiff, my shoes are tight and stiff. I itch.

Mother squares her shoulders. *Sit up. Sit still.*
She smiles, purses her lips. *Close your mouth.*

For My Birthday

My father shows me how
to hold the whetstone,

how a knife trusts the tyrant
of a hand. I practice how

the edge can nick my nail.
We carve a propeller curved,

angled, blades matched by eye.
Don't take too much at once,

you can't go back, he says
and drills the spindle hole.

I spin it high. Dandelion
float, sideways drift,

our little helicopter
threatening nothing.

Paper Planes

Folded from *Time*'s cover, narrow-winged,
mine, stiff, red, right-angled symmetry

fell from the porch like a feathered bomb.
My brother used black and white

news of the war in Spain, crayonned
blue bullseyes on the heraldic wings
that never plunged, hovering over earth

unrolling like a painted movie backdrop
where freewheeling trees and houses

moved one way while the Sherman tank
stood still facing another, waging war.

Good Work

I never knew his name. When he snapped
a chamois in air once, twice, a shoe would shine

like the armor of the company of knights
in my picture book of knights. Each Sunday

before church he came to sit mute
in our front hall, his tired box squatting

on the fire of the cool red tiles that lit
the morning, shoes gathered by my father

from our closets to give the man his work.
I'd crouch and watch, the way I watched

my father lather up to shave, and if
my Sunday best were there I'd pay

from my own pocket my own two coins.

Making a Map

Playing god at the dining table
upon a sheet of paper
vast as a polar ice-cap

my brother and I divide
water from land with pencils
We join shorelines

label cities in the news
Narvik   Danzig   Dunkirk
Skopje   Salonika   Pec

his black squares   my black
circles   linked by red
for railroads at the blue border

We grow jealous of tree lines
fighting   now   for space
in the world we have made

Taxi Driver

All Deeb sees I see
purple iris   a mountain coat
of arms   goats cluttering

the road   stones clattering
the mudguards   every wolf
that used to be   He lets me sit

in front beside the gear shift
for luck   blue camel beads
swinging from the rear view

mirror in which his mouth
is talking Arabic   We stop
at the sign of a Red Horse

flying   He pumps blue gas
dusts the dash and crested
hood   leaving time behind

The Wild Iris

War driving us away
My father sets free

his only hybrid
digs the rhizome
shaped like a ginger root

hires Deeb to drive him
to Kniesse's dusty

goat road   climbs
to the very spot
where iris flourish

takes from his knapsack
the yellow bloom

trowels a hole
spreads the roots
heaps the dirt

and tamps it down
The taxi waits

Leaving Beirut

April 30, 1941, no idea what lies ahead.
                                                    –My mother's diary

May 3, Iraq and Britain at war,
all foreign students sent home.
Goodbye summer   tennis   goodbye

softball   Feisal's soda fountain
mother rationing sugar   chocolate
whipped cream   ice cream sundaes

to eat in the garden behind high walls
Our cook Adeebi rattles breakfast
I love Wheatena   She's staying

with my books on the shelf and the cat
who can walk to Palestine
by himself if he chooses

May 15, Germans coming in large numbers.
There will be searchlights   Goodbye
banyan   goodbye Barouk cedars

May 18, tension, trunks
to leave behind.   Distant drone
my suitcase packed for weeks

May 19, we leave tomorrow
at 8:30.   Refugee taxi comes
headlights painted blackout blue

We're going to Jerusalem
the church's silver grotto

June 8, troops entered Syria at 2 a.m.
We're going to the Dead Sea
float like hot bubbles

June 12, chicken pox.   No more school
Hurrah   Sister counts my brother's
180 scabs   I count my 49

June 15, Egyptian consulate.
We're going to the pyramids by camel

June 22, Damascus falls.   I find a coin
We see *The Thief of Baghdad*

July 28, Today we learn our sailing date.
Goodbye U-boats   goodbye Monopoly
albatross at sunset   sandcastle wars

July 29, awful humidity.
Past bedtime airplanes soar steep
gray like kites   We're crossing Cairo

by taxi   angry at traffic   Father's jacket
smells of mountains   He's going home
Goodbye to mountains

Postcard from the Grand Canyon

OCT 9 8AM 1941
Dear Dad We have had
a very nice day here This morning

a ladder scaled the watchtower
at Desert View a million
purple-valley shadows

a little creek winding down
a little way *we took a bus ride*
to Hermits Rest vague as the Painted

Desert's flat line I was a fruit fly
on the rim *stopping at several places*
like the far side of the moon

to take in the view the geese
occupied with black ants and fire
ants sunk in the marl

campgrounds of guy ropes
and pegs the layer-cake cliffs
The colors were very nice

Uranus the Zodiac spun round
Polaris an uncertain heirarchy
silence complete *Love Allen*

Playing across America

Out the window horses gallop   Slanty sun
blinds the signs   Gallup NM   Grade crossings
on the Staked Plain   sagebrush waves heaving

the horizon like ocean swells   Up and down
the ladders of our new life   we lie low
behind green curtains   beneath our berths

in and out of dark   Tom Mix and Lash Larue
wield ivory-gripped pistols aboard the Grand
Canyon Limited   my sister zinging make-believe

arrows from an Indian bow   straws in her hair
hawk feathers   Jump up   *bang*   fall down
bang   The sandwich man   white jacket and hat

holds a tray blocking the aisle   We buy American
and mustard on *Wonder*   our first *Baby Ruth*
bars and *Coca Cola*   Amarillo   *Burma Shave*

Clovis   The *ABC* game   Refugees
our Pullman a ship   we dare each other
to slip   to fall   the seats lifeboats   leap

the aisles full of sharks   my brother
hanging on   my sister's ruthless fling
one sneaker lost under the keel

II. BASIC TRAINING

Fenway Park

Homesick for earth, that ball rides the roar
of all the fedoras and Army caps

over the shortstop's self-centered confidence,
the left fielder, casual in the technical grass,

over the big green wall, blue fumes and beer,
the game in extra innings. What's wrong

with the sun up there, a crescent question
behind a cirrus veil? My body doesn't have

an answer, my father a month away —
Tobruk! Benghazi! Tock! of bat — by airmail.

X-Rays

Acned in a scientific chair,
I watch the ceiling fan spin

like a fighter plane's lazy propeller,
wear a lead blanket up to my chin.

The machine's hum excites hope.
At the school dance my good suit

was all wrong, livid, the blue tweed
rough as a herringbone out of date.

Something was wrong with my tie.
What girl would have clung to me?

Terse Biography of My Father

Self-control froze him,
mouth tight, eyes wary,
ten and his father

already dead. I was ten
when war spread
oceans between him

in Beirut and me
wrapped in shyness,
a fragile package

roughly tied with twine
whose knots I pick.
When we meet again,

no words
for love, which comes
as no surprise.

Prep School Vacation

Sheltered by clustering pines
that crowd the hill, I laze

in the sleeping shack, wooden
box with clerestory windows,

brass bed, shelf for eyeglasses
and flashlight, gaunt wooden

chair, my scarred suitcase.
Afternoons, quiet heat, time

to read: *A Study in Scarlet,*
Tess of the D'Urbervilles.

Soon Orion and the Pleiades
will burn and flashlights

flicker from the paths
like fireflies. *Forever Amber.*

Houseparty Weekend

May is hung
with Japanese lanterns,
crimson globes

suffusing girls in white
dresses and us, the men

of suits, white shirts.
At the garden party
I stand alone, now

pawn, now king, move
to the punch bowl

one square at a time,
crushing the little yellow
potentillas underfoot.

Dear Three,

Sunday mornings our mother layers
two sheets of carbon paper shiny side

down among onion-skin, three leaves,
feeds them to the Underwood perfectly

aligned for each of us, fingers playing
the keyboard vivace, click-click-clack,

each week her typos, her crossings-out.
On the back of my letter sharp dents

of periods and commas etch a bas-relief
of braille, and squeezed onto the bottom

of the page for each of us, *Mom* in blue
ink witnesses news of home as from

a war zone, the stamps on the envelope
perfectly franked. *red anemones*

out everywhere and cyclamen . . .

Camp Gordon, Georgia

1

They're still fighting in Korea.
I am US51188632, lose myself
to confidence, learn to perform

rifle rituals, earn medals,
Marksman, Sharpshooter,
those bullseyes, edges ripped,

lead-smeared, my Garand
infinitely lethal, gas-operated,
semi-automatic, ten rounds

lock and load. *Observe*
yourself as if it's tennis
you're playing, synchrony

of arms, geometry choosing
the angles. It was my father
showed me the sweet spot

on my racket, force barely
needed once I got it right,
the little steps, a shuffle

that put me in position.
Don't let the muzzle wander.
Breathe in calmly the powder-

flavored smoke, breathe it out,
keep the sight steady
on the black. . . . Squeeze.

2

trucked all day
       mucked up
  shot at   dug down
  saturated   just settled

    the pup tent   cold
     as a january grave

pack up! the lieutenant shouts
    five minutes
and we roll! trucks
   revving   stuff
  the sleeping bag in the duffel
    pull the pegs
     roll them
  in the tent   tied
with its own ropes
       that bastard
    shakes us
  up like molecules
in a flask   isomerizes
       our bonds

i should have stayed
    with chemistry paid

attention to the bayonet
instructor   sergeant first class
        cabral   was there

                                        a target

        in prison camp
    in forty-two   what if
            the panic's real   they told us
    we might go any day

Spring with Two Crows

They dodge   dive
roll   tails flaring
steering   a World

War I dogfight
with love
instead of bullets

They loop the sky
at dusk
inextricably

entwined   end up
side by side
overhead   ripening

silent   Daylight
shrinks like earth
in drought

Leave beauty
to the tongue
and hold me

In a Slow Elevator

winter was hard
come up for a drink

she says   her silk skirt
clinging like wind-blown

leaves   a spinning
implacable flight path

thank god for rain
she says

time to fear   time
to hope   rain's

passion   earth's need
the fifth-floor blue

glass door shows up
iron arabesques

embedded fisheye
stay   she says

The Lighter

With callused thumb I spin
the little wheel that sparks

the flame to which she flies
beguiled, bright-winged, eyes

blue as a song in a smoky lounge,
Pall Mall caught by puckered

lips that leave a fierce red print.
She'll give up smoking for hand

and mouth, the apparatus
of desire. Oh the tango

we dance, the orange blossom
I sip from her smile.

Free Verse

Anything
we want it to be
our voices stumbling
the pitch-black road
that suddenly seisms
tilting you toward me
my arm
across your shoulders

the moon's
empty bowl dropped
behind a scrim of hills
the stars'
wild spill dizzying
Humming Gershwin
we climb off the map
to a new language

verbs so tense
they have no voice
Outside our room
you hand me the key
Above the lawn
a bat is dancing
white moths into
out of the light

Touch

Everyone knows
who takes me to bed

single-minded   hungry
I used to chase the sand's

raw gapes   its cusps
of foam   the skipping

sand fleas
what they need I need

In the long grass
blue plums blush

Along the shore eiders
flock in rafts   wide

bodies calm as dories
stable as decoys   Oh

to be one of them
their down

against my skin

I Didn't Say Enough

The fragile year when love became
self-conscious, your indignant voice
between our rusty highs and lows
left shadows of mistrust unsolved.

Self-conscious your indignant voice,
the depth of you, too deep for me,
left shadows of mistrust unsolved,
my heart a mute and trembling wall.

The depth of you too deep for me,
Talk to me before you think, you said,
my heart a mute and trembling wall.
I caught fire, plumbed your words,

Talk to me before you think, you said,
find the spaces, let them breathe.
I caught fire, plumbed your words,
lines wrote themselves and trusted,

found the spaces, let them breathe
between our rusty highs and lows.
Lines wrote themselves and trusted
the fragile year when love became.

Tea Ritual

There is something
about heat   viscosity

anticipation   On the porch
beside a brown clay pot

our mugs sit   sepia pigs
on mine   all around

the cylinder of hers
blue rabbits dancing

Words are irrelevant
We take for granted a duet

of rests   stops and starts
and at the steeped end

whatever brews in the pot
sugars our desire

Paradox

Big stones need two men
to lift, carry, crowbar into place,
keep the raw hillside still, settle
as comfortable as sleep.

To lift, carry, crowbar into place
what will become
as comfortable as sleep,
my father and I make

what will become
a wall, solid three-dimensioned.
My father and I make
a jigsaw puzzle of stones,

a wall, solid three-dimensioned,
Where does this go?
a jigsaw puzzle of stones,
Which comes next? Surrogates,

Where does this go?
what we cannot say.
Which comes next? Surrogates
of conversation. And who knew

what we cannot say
against red clay
of conversation? And who knew,
enclosing the day

against red clay,
stones break down walls?
Enclosing the day,
we build and rebuild each other.

Stones break down walls,
keep the raw hillside still, settle.
We build and rebuild each other,
two men who need big stones.

The Rope

The Blue Ridge and the pines
his heaven, he hiked the long hill —
a knapsack for bread, milk, bananas —

until feet went numb, then folded
the tent of his world into a house
of iron silence, his face closed, teeth

lost. No one to ask for pills. All day
at the window counting the seeds
in the feeder. Night. He was reading

Durrell, *Bitter Lemons* under pooled
lamplight, the clock in the dark — *two,*
then *three.* How did he scale

those attic stairs, legs insensate
as the olivewood walking sticks
he made? He couldn't feel

the shoes on his feet. I forgive
that rope he heaved, dragged
taut over the beam.

Harvest

The season is late
rain not enough
to fill the cisterns

wet the gasping fields
snow not enough
to feed limestone

rifts and springs
that feed the crops

Let rain burst the clouds
Let drifts bury high
the mountains deep

Let muddy beneficence
like saintly snakes
coil the orchards

apricot   almond
pomegranate   fig

The Green Years

Arabic, my father's second language,
spoke to common things of childhood:
the back of a mule, quiet village

women who walked as calm as water
in the earthenware jars they filled
at the '*ain* and balanced home to rest

on racks of rough pine planks.
Near a den in oregano's wild hillside,
where pine-tree summers slept

and pooled green cups of spring
tempted him with fretwork paths,
he found a young vixen, tamed her

with love and chicken bones until
she would curl on his lap, then run
and run the garden, chased by the dog

who always ended in the rosebush
at the long path's end, just when she
jumped sideways never to be caught.

Pilgrim

The man beside me smiles. We shrug
in Lebanese. Home, my Mecca, blue

luggage riding the carousel. I have come
to dream the banyan, the jackals, the castle

ramparts, the wild perfume of goats
conjured up, hail a cab to College Gate,

roll my suitcase three blocks
to the schoolhouse, terminus of laundry,

roof tiles red as tulips that bloom
and vanish before wheat. Olive groves

hang on, hands rebuild the rebuilt
peaceable houses, stone upon stone

upon stone. On the cliffs above the River
of the Dog carved boasts of conquerers

erode — Ramses, Sennacherib. I sleep.
I wake. I have come incognito,

my neighborhood concrete, indifferent,
bullet-strafed, uneasy the longing,

the jagged basking minarets. Clouds go
on and on. No one's come for me.

III. IN A TIME OF RIPE FIGS

For they had lived together long enough to know that love was always love, anytime and anyplace, but it was more solid the closer it came to death.

– Gabriel García Márquez

The River's Edge

The dog is impatient
for the scent of lilacs. When
did her bad dream start?

Buds bloat the rhododendron,
the berry bush knee-deep
in dusty blue swells.

A swelling is what wakes you
when it hurts too much.
Yesterday the vet

palpated the dog's belly.
Nothing in there, he said.
Today she runs by the river

where purple iris wave
and wither. I plant basil,
water the tomatoes.

She leans against me
                hungry.

Ten-Pin

I was a healed scar, didn't itch
until the shock. Now blood cakes
under my fingernails, wind makes me
its instrument, a wooden whistle,
and the song has different words,

changed rhythms, a minor key,
feelings the same, never the same.
IVs are bittersweet, measured
poison strangling her stone-white.

Time takes forever to run
fast, plows the future ahead,
piles it like snow, circles back,
and bowls me into a heap.

Everything Is Happening Again

You gave me back
your wedding ring.

I keep it in my coin purse,
and the days relapse:

Enter   Do Not Enter
on glass doors, voices

choking the voicemail, stale
news wrinkling the waiting

room. Climbing the tower
behind a stony shine, elevators

hide their hearts, and pumps
are hooked to your drowsing,

the view from the bed
the same, except the trees.

Even If It Might

Because we knew
it wouldn't because
it already had
we were beyond
everything but talk
even if it
wouldn't   even if
it might know
too much we
did not know
only fruit trembling
a little   rumor
and the words

I Comforted Her with Apples

I comforted her with apples
bending the garnet
branches   I climbed

picked them into the curve
of skirt she lifted
following me

under the trees   intent
silent   looking up   Let go
they bounced   bruising

the stones   She knelt
to her gathering   cider
all they were good for

Solitaire

I've begun to walk head down
as if each found coin bought
a day   better yet a month

Under yews   around the trash
as if each scrap could assuage her
the dog snaps apple cores
sniffs   jerks the leash
leaves frantic wet replies

At home I find you shuffling
dealing solitaire   as if
remission were in the cards

Pas de Deux

My bath
                    How long since that scent
hot rose geranium   inviting
                    promised your body
as always   My body
                    your body and I can't look
has become grotesque
                    yet from the back
I can do it
                    your torso smiles   hips
I loathe
                    smooth bulbs on the curved
giving up   ashamed
                    candelabrum of your spine
to have you see
                    All the looks
my bony shoulders
                    that ever touched you
my belly
                    grow within you

After Breakfast

She irons
my handkerchiefs
unstitches needlepoint
the unicorn caught

within its fence
on her pillow
in the living room
her head bent   bald

all her scars inside
She has tamed
the winds of panic
does what she has to

or asks me to
so I bring *the red dress*
without a waist I bought
for summer   knee socks

the new loafers
                her cranberry
red wool coat
Walking   she's breathless

Let the slope have been
steeper than it seemed
When I go back will they
bring a cart?

              Let me
always
have loved her like this

The Tumbler

My deceitful poems paper her
over   hiding from all of you how
she yanked the blanket to her

side   had to have the last word
about money   where to plant
rhubarb   gave advice in triplicate

collected catalogs   *Land's End   Hold*
Everything   Winter Silks   piled
hamper-deep   how she ordered

another go-round with Gevalia
coffee   another clutch
of panty-hose

Her singing drifted slightly flat
She didn't like going out
after dark   shied from small-talk

at cocktail parties   hated
movies   hated TV   I didn't
notice how the red plastic

tumbler filled itself
with bourbon

False Dawn

I've been working
the odds forever   Last night
nothing was right   nothing
I did   nothing I didn't   In bed
her hands were cold   I scuffled
for words   This morning
winter grips
ice armoring the window
where she stands
sectioning two grapefruit
halves   on the radio
it's nineteen thirty-nine
Yehudi Menuhin playing
Bloch's violin concerto
making the notes
into a scream

Amber

White-silence
resigned   white
nightgown   shivering
flannel   lavender

flowers white-faced
her hands white marble
I arrange in a calm
green bowl

a small sweet melon
two black plums
The sun moves

a shadow up the wall
Everything is
what it is beside the bed
Her pills

are exhausted
                    By dawn
they will stop
pretending

beloved

your wrist is still
as warm as an egg

in my palm
i dare not touch

your pale leached
ear   dare not taste

your lips
your cracked tongue's

charred underside
i do not see your dreams

do not enter your bed
but bend to you

inhale the broken
breath

When I get home I

kneel on living room floor   slit tape with my pocket
knife   pull off top of blue cardboard box   take plastic
bag out of box   untwist the green twist-em
                                                    weigh bag
on bathroom scale   six pounds of gray ash   powdery
as raw cement mixed with chunks of bone
                                                    spoon some
into empty coffee tin to take to Cataumet   pick up
bag   tip it into box   gently shake out ash   toss
bag into step-on can   smell ash   put box on table
                                                    find
a wide roll of tape on the third shelf in back hall
                                                    take
kitchen scissors from knife block   cut tape   seal box
lay down scissors   put box under my arm   grab shovel
push open back door   climb down four steps
                                                    lay box
beside the laurel   dig a hole   put box in earth
                                                    let it rot

I Find Her

With a silver dime on the bottom
of her brocade purse   Among Kleenex

crumpled up both sleeves
of her kimono crawling with blue dragons

In her bureau's empty box of Egyptian
cigarettes and a tangle of brassieres

that caught and cup my lost handkerchief
In the top left-hand drawer

of little bottles   *Chanel   Arpège*
Obsession that scented her bath

when I loved her body
the way it plumbed
                              the long deep tub

Black Bag

Bag after trash bag I fill   pressing out the air
suffocating heels and toes   so many shoes

a boiled wool jacket   its bone buttons   a down
pillow's puffy hedge   Tied up   all those bags

I carry down   throw them over the tailgate
of the Subaru   a dark mountain of next-to-new

I'm cleaning out as if moving into a place
I've never been before, but here the doorbell

rang at two a.m. and I couldn't help watching
the red-faced man unmake the bottom sheet

wrap her   spread a black bag beside her
on the bed   lift her   feet first   then shoulders

zip it   heave the sack of roots onto the gurney
strap it tight   I helped him bounce it down

the steps   load it into the black car's blacker
yawn   the wet night empty   Nothing shone

My Heart

Do I not trot
a treadmill for you
listen to the skips stop

when you speed up
Distraught over everyday
you rouse for effort

for love when night chokes
on weeds   *fleurs du mal*
fleurs de la bel

The cold moon alone
can whip your breaking
and I do not sleep

until you beat away
the owl that hunts me
and the great griffon

At the Fountain

Green overhangs the jet
Duckling doesn't

understand my mind
scurries edge

to edge   poised
to ignite glittering

the reckless rhythms
of water   Oh

to strip naked   fling
into that cold antidote

heat   hunger
obsession

Ghost

Leave the restless bed
and swim across the cove
toward somewhere
warmer than air   shore
blacker than reflection
If a beach looms
and your fingers stroke
the sandy bottom
keep the moon
on your left to guide you
in the dark   your face
turning into and out of
the water
      Life narrows down
I can't tell how far
you have to go

Summer

Sunrise cutting sleep
casual meals at inscrutable
hours   I repeated

the names of the months
over and over to hold
my mind   comforted

by the tide chart on the wall
worried who would be
in the sandwich shop at noon

or what it would serve
that I could bring myself to eat
Autumn came   I fled back

to bus schedules   and despite
crowds and irrational potholes
the city's grid steadied me

Down the Street of Sleep

Four hours deep in the sweet
of it   my feet relaxed as toast

If at three I remember
the butterfly dream   or even
if I don't   I'm still entitled

to get up   raise the blind   see
whether the pond is frozen or not
It is   The night's been fractured

the day a pot of tea   I look out
the window   standing
in my nightshirt   When I peel

it off   drop it into the machine
with white socks   underwear
a wool red hat   everything

will come out pink   I rather like
pink   shut the lid   dial gentle   sit
in the kitchen wearing my love's

too-tight cashmere sweater
still perfumed   my tea stronger
more bitter   *Who have I been?*

Making Jelly Alone

Behind the sirens
and a jet's faint buzz

I pick clean the grapes
that rattle my steel bowl

like grapeshot   skins
powder-blue as old jeans

the stems full of spiders
We used to gather wild grapes

by the bucket   stripped
them side-by-side   strained

through cheesecloth
a dozen jars of tart juice

Aubade

From the close-cropped field
a silken donkey comes
with all her gray economy
ears turned to my voice   leans over
the fence   bends calm-eyed
to me   muzzle white
as summer that fills the valley
I soothe the mouth that snuffs
and the forehead where the terrible
fly bites itch   This morning
suddenly I desire to rub
the small of your back
I used to kiss

Poem for My Birthday

Blackberries   a wild tangle
steaming somnolent
ripe   drunk as a birthday
with fermenting
These I harvest
bloody-thumbed until
my pail is full   the dog
lipping all she can reach
among the thorns

One black redstart flutters
the parapet   a lizard
scales the sun-warmed wall

like a god of summer
A woman passes
dressed in flowers
What lifts her heart
Church bells purl
morning like water
rocks and river
the same going   coming
I am not what I was

About the Changes
and So Much More Unchanged

Tadpoles   water-boatmen
naiads   Does it matter?
Dragonflies   a drowse

of butterflies   Brambles
interdict the path
Hornets of childhood

dangerous still
distill their honey
underground

The time of ripe figs
is beginning   I am happy

compost turned
by an unimagined blade

Dancing While Sweeping

Surreal comes tonight
  in the eyes of a cat
    and the broom's used beauty

Without white tie
  or tails   I am
    Fred Astaire naked

star-stuff
  as lonely
    as Polaris immobile

sing *La Paloma*
  drape on the broom
    her lavender robe

one sleeve lifted high
  one over my shoulders
    Arpège-scented silk

clings   never missing
  a beat   holds me
    my need to be

held   Our dipping
  and turning shape
    circles and gyres

embracing my heaven
   of table lamps
      floor lamps

enchanting our tango
   The wide-open back door
      welcomes our dust

Allen West, born in Beirut, Lebanon, in 1930, came to the U.S. with his family after the 1941 invasion of Greece by Germany. Educated at Phillips Academy and Princeton University, he served three years in the U.S. Army and received a Ph.D. in chemistry from Cornell University in 1960. He taught at Williams College and Lawrence University until 1994, when he and his wife Emily moved to Cambridge, Massachusetts. While there, he was a tutor at Cambridge Rindge & Latin High School and a volunteer at Recording for the Blind & Dyslexic. His wife died in 1999; he has three children and three grandchildren.

He began writing poetry in 1983. A runner-up for the 1992 *Grolier Poetry Prize* and winner of the *White Eagle Coffee Store Press*'s 2000 chapbook competition ("The Time of Ripe Figs," published in 2002), his poems have appeared in many journals including *Passager, The Comstock Review, Concrete Wolf, RHINO, and Salamander.* A long-time member of The Workshop for Publishing Poets in Brookline, Massachusetts, he credits his continued development to its director, Barbara Helfgott Hyett. Since 2007 he has lived in Lexington, Massachusetts.